To Carol

Do This!

Mary

Also by Mary LoVerde

Stop Screaming at the Microwave!
How to Connect Your Disconnected Life

Touching Tomorrow

HOW TO INTERVIEW YOUR LOVED ONES
TO CAPTURE A LIFETIME OF MEMORIES
ON VIDEO OR AUDIO

Mary LoVerde

A Fireside Book
Published by Simon & Schuster
New York   London   Toronto   Sydney

FIRESIDE
Rockefeller Center
1230 Avenue of the Americas
New York, NY 10020

Designed by William P. Ruoto

Manufactured in the United States of America

3 5 7 9 10 8 6 4

Library of Congress Cataloging-in-Publication Data is available

ISBN 0-684-87380-X

An earlier edition of this work was published in 1998 as
Your Family's Greatest Gift

This book is dedicated to:

My parents, Tom and Lou Schulte,
who gave me the greatest gift,
a sense of belonging

Sister Mary Ellen Schulte,
who models for all of us a loving respect for the elderly

Esther LoVerde,
my inspiration for this book

With a special dedication in memory of Kay Czarnecki,
my friend and incredible graphic designer

Acknowledgments

I have been researching the ideas for this project for eight years. At each step of my discovery process, someone appeared to show me what I needed to learn. I want to especially thank:

Jillian Manus, my agent. You are always there for me. How lucky can a writer get?

Marah Stets, my editor, who stepped right up to the plate and made this happen. What a pleasure it is to work with you.

Becky Cabaza, my first editor, who knows exactly how to get the best work out of me. I am so grateful for the joy you brought into my life.

Robert Miller, the truest of friends. I love sharing our passion for creating.

Roswitha Smale, one of my mentors, who gave me the idea for the interview in the first place. You are so generous with your wisdom and time.

Connie Asher, Diane Graves, and Katie McKenna of Asher Studio, who generously worked with me to keep this project alive.

Judy Anderson, my longtime friend and internationally renowned graphic designer, who believed in the idea and designed the original concept.

Pat Riley of the Allen Tate company, who titled the book. I am forever in your debt.

Wes Hempel, the most creative person I know, who taught me five years' worth of writing in one class.

David Miller, who came out of nowhere to give me brilliant suggestions that I would never have come up with in a million years.

Jonellen Heckler, my favorite author. Thank you for encouraging me to find my own voice. I admire you so!

Lou Heckler, who sent me the question, "What is the greatest gift a family can give itself?" I am so blessed to know you.

Jim Estey, who helped me pioneer my ideas. You taught me an enormous amount about my own project by sharing your experience and insights, and by being such a good listener.

Barbara and Rod Romig, who live in one of the most beautiful places on earth and unbelievably let me stay at their Hawaiian home while I wrote this book.

Lynn Price, founder of Camp To Belong. You have a beautiful soul and an important mission. I am thrilled to be a part of your adventure.

Mark Camacho and Ben Cover of Video Engage-ments, who edited my parents' video so beautifully. If only you knew what joy you've brought to our family because of your talent and professionalism.

Mary Jones, the inventor. You are unstoppable when you get an idea in your head.

My Chapman University students and all my friends and family who helped me research the best questions to ask. You always come through for me.

My mastermind members: Melanie Mills, Scott Friedman, Brian O'Malley, Mark Sanborn, Eric Chester, and Brenda Abdilla. You urge me to live my mission by your marvelous example. I am honored to be among you.

Mary and Rolf Benirschke, who have demon-strated time and again what perseverance, family, and faith are all about. What an inspiration you are to me!

Barbara Lubbers, my friend and trainer. You stim-ulate my creativity so much I may have to make you a coauthor.

Sam Horn, my gentle genius friend. Please keep teaching me.

Sheri Krug, my assistant. How nice of the Universe to send you to me!

Brenda Abdilla, my dearest friend. It took me a long time to find you. What would I do without you?

My parents, Tom and Lou Schulte, and my brothers Tom, Jr.; Bob; Bill; Greg; and Chuck, who so patiently support my whacky ideas. I love you.

With love to Joe, Sarah, Emily, and Nicholas. I look forward to touching tomorrow with all of you!

Touching
Tomorrow

Contents

❧

Foreword

In the scope of wonderment and reality, *Touching Tomorrow* invites you and your family to relive the unforgettable memories of their lifetimes. Treat yourself to a journey of cheers and tears as you weave a family video heirloom to share with future generations.

The setting is what you make it. The presentation of the questions is who you are and what you want to learn about your family. In a simple question format, with tips to ensure the completeness of this unique gift to yourself and others, you will discover and understand the important, and often times hidden, special secrets as you reminisce with those who mean the most to you.

In family and in friendship, you will share and feel a true sense of fulfillment of learning about your heritage. Mary LoVerde has given us the inspiring opportunity to draw out the precious and enduring moments of those we love.

Touching Tomorrow will be a treasure to hold close in heart and spirit.

—Lynn Price, founder, Camp To Belong

Introduction

※

TOUCHING TOMORROW:
MOVING THE LEGACY FORWARD

*Call it a clan, call it a network, call it a tribe,
call it a family, whatever you call it, whoever
you are, you need one.*

—Jane Howard

Congratulations! You are about to create a legacy of memories for your family and friends. I've designed this book to show you, step-by-step, how to interview your loved ones and audio- or videotape the conversation, resulting in a treasured family heirloom. It is very easy to do; however, it does take some preparation. But remember this: the efforts you give now will enrich the lives of generations to come. No tangible gift could be more valuable.

YOUR FAMILY'S GREATEST GIFT

In writing this book, I surveyed hundreds of people about the questions they wanted to ask their parents or grandparents. Not one person turned me down! Everyone, it seemed, had unanswered questions. What were their parents' earliest recollections? What were they like as teenagers? What was their greatest accomplishment? What single event taught them an important lesson? What made their marriage work?

Robert Akeret, author of *Family Tales, Family Wisdom,* wrote that he, too, has never met a person who did not want to know more about his parents' and grandparents' lives. He said, "Wanting to understand who our parents really are, wanting to grasp the whole sweep of their lives, from childhood to old age, is a fundamental curiosity. And for very good reason. Because we know intuitively that what shaped their lives has shaped our lives, too."

The questions people sent me illustrated the richness of family history. "Grandma, what was it like to be a picture bride?" "What was life like during the Great Depression?" "What was it like being at home while the men were away at war?"

One of my mentors, Lou Heckler, sent me a particularly interesting question. He asked, "What is the greatest gift a family can give itself?" The question haunted me. I wanted the answer. For certainly whatever it was, I wanted my family to have it.

My obvious answer was love. But not all families love each other, I reasoned, at least not all the time. So if love wasn't the answer, what was it? Why is it true that whoever you are, and whether you love them or not, you need a family? Psychologists would tell us the family fills our most basic need: to belong—to feel a connection to others. And that, I believe, is the greatest gift a family can give itself—a sense of belonging, a sense of knowing who our family is.

When I went to my ninety-six-year-old grandmother's funeral, the church was packed with people, most of us related in some way. I was overwhelmed with the sense of family that enveloped me. I realized that Grandma Schulte had offered us the greatest gift a family can give itself. We all belonged to her and to each other.

Modern times can strain our sense of belonging. Television, voice mail, faxes, e-mail, and the World Wide Web—we could live much of our lives without any human connection. Our mobile society, divorce and remarriage, and the changing economic times complicate our lives and only amplify our need for family ties.

In "the good ole days" families spent hours listening to their elders tell stories, passing family history and wisdom to the next generation. Critics charge that television and the Web have silenced many families. But we can use this technology now to bring families together again. Imagine watching your parents or grandparents star in their own show, sharing their special feelings and memories with those they love, right on your own TV or Web site!

IT'S ALL ABOUT BALANCE

We all want more balanced lives. We have been managing, organizing, delegating, simplifying, and juggling until we are black and blue. For many of us these strategies have disconnected us from those we love and how we really want our lives to be. In our zeal "to get it all done" we have ignored sources of wisdom that are right in front of us. My life's work is summed up in the sentence: Connection creates balance. In my first book, *Stop Screaming at the Microwave! How to Connect Your Disconnected Life*, I wrote about specific strategies to stay connected with yourself, your family and friends, and your spirituality. I related stories about the incredible connections I created in my own family by videotaping interviews with my parents and in-laws. I received a flood of letters. "How can I do this project for my family? What questions do I ask? How do I master the videotaping or audiotape recording? What will it cost? Please send help—now!"

This book is the answer to those letters. I believe that you will find more balance in your life by doing this project than any fancy Day-Timer will ever give you. You will rediscover old connections and create new ones. You will feel good.

And feeling good is what life balance is all about.

WHY TOMORROW?

I am passionate about helping you create a way to move your family's legacy forward because I have experienced firsthand, with my own family, how much it can change your life. So many people have written to me to say, "You are right! Our family does feel like we have touched tomorrow." How does this work?

Tomorrow you will be closer to your loved ones because of what you discover.

Tomorrow you will use that knowledge to be a better daughter, son, parent, grandparent, relative, or friend.

Tomorrow you will understand who you are just a little bit better.

Tomorrow you will feel a deeper respect and forgive and forget more easily.

Tomorrow your elder will feel honored that you cared enough to ask.

Tomorrow you will comfort yourself by reliving the memories long after your loved one is gone.

*Tomorrow you will share your loved one's wisdom with
   generations to come.*

*And tomorrow those generations will pass it down as
   well.*

Lillian Lindner, the mother of a friend of mine,
wrote a beautiful piece called "Lillian's Laws for
Living," a simple bit of wisdom that so moved me
that I asked her permission to publish it in *Stop
Screaming at the Microwave!* She penned her ideas as a
way to move her own legacy forward. After Lillian's
death her daughter, Jaye Lunsford, wrote to me to
say how much it meant to her mother that her ideas
were published. She said, "I think we all want to
leave a tangible gift behind. My mother told all the
doctors and nurses about her inclusion in your
book. I know it made her dying a little easier to
know that her words would live on." I was thrilled to
learn that Lillian and I had joined forces so that she
could touch tomorrow.

HOW TO USE THIS BOOK

I designed this book to be used by both the interviewer and the interviewee. I have carefully crafted
The Interview (page 87), printed in large typed text
on easy-to-photocopy pages so each family member
can participate. The Interview includes a series of

questions that will cover each stage of life as well as some specially selected questions to help you capture the essence of who your loved one really is. I also encourage you to customize the questions for your family member. You may select from the list of additional questions that I have provided or create your own. For example, I asked my father where he was and how he felt on VJ Day. I asked my stylish mother about her favorite outfit. You may also ask the interviewee and other family members and friends for questions. I gave my list of questions to my parents and asked them to circle or cross out their preferences. I was surprised and pleased with the questions they really wanted to answer.

While many of the questions will evoke serious and heartfelt responses, don't forget to be playful. I asked both my parents what "naughty" things they had done as teenagers. They delighted in recalling their mischievous antics. (My mother locked the high school principal out on the balcony!) In my question survey, one respondent wrote that he would ask his father, "Dad, will you tell us about the time you streaked through that hardware store?" If this is true for your relative, be sure to ask!

The number of questions is not important, but do try to cover all of life's stages. To help with the recall, I suggest you give this book to your relative (or make a photocopy of the questions), one to two weeks before the scheduled interview so they can review the questions and begin reminiscing. Before the interview, discuss the questions you'll ask. Then use this book as your tool for planning and executing the interview. You can use The Interview just as it is written or write your own choices on the lines provided for you on each page. It is also helpful to use those lines to write yourself notes. For example, I wrote "Dad's first bicycle" by the question asking for childhood memories. Be sure to include your notes on the photocopy of the interview questions you give your relative.

The book is divided into six parts:

PART ONE: OVERCOMING RESISTANCE

What to do when the wall goes up. You'll learn ways to "sell" the idea to reluctant loved ones, making it easy for them to say yes.

PART TWO: TELLING THE TALES AND CAPTURING THE WISDOM

How to conduct a fun-filled, heartwarming interview. You'll get valuable ideas on how to help your loved one recall a rich treasure of memories. You will unlock the door to the values, the opinions, and the wisdom built through years of real-life experiences.

PART THREE: RECORDING THE JOURNEY

Videotaping and audiotape recording tips, editing ideas, and cost considerations. This section is the nuts and bolts of how to make your family heirloom a reality, chock-full of practical ideas that will delight and reassure you.

PART FOUR: RECALLING A LIFE

The time-tested interview with questions that will result in a video or audiotape that will delight the whole family, including the interviewee. The questions are designed to give your loved ones an opportunity to reflect on their lives and the lives of those they love. Just ask the questions and wait to be amazed.

PART FIVE: MAKING IT UNIQUELY YOUR OWN

An array of thought-provoking questions that you can use to customize your interview. Your family is one of a kind. Select from one hundred sixty additional questions to make your interview reflect your family's uniqueness or use them to stimulate your own questions. Your loved one can review the questions and select those that seem fitting. You may be very surprised at what they choose. You will find questions that will lead you into areas you may have never before discussed with your relatives.

PART SIX: CREATING A LIVING LINK

The hidden benefits of this project, today and tomorrow.

Although the focus is on the end product, you may be thrilled with all the additional benefits that many families have gained through the process. Your family's children, teens, and adults deserve to hear what your elders have to say about life's most important issues—work, love, parenthood, community, regrets, and rewards. It's something they can't learn anywhere else. You will be amazed at the new connections that are created.

Woven throughout the book you will find two additional features: Variation boxes, detailing innovative ways to take these ideas in a new direction; and In Real Life boxes, letters from people who have completed their interviews and wanted to inspire and encourage you with their experience.

It is my hope that this book will make interviewing your loved one fun and easy, and that it will give you laughter and tears, insight, and wisdom. But most of all, I hope it gives you and yours the greatest gift a family can give itself—that wonderful, irreplaceable, all-encompassing sense of belonging.

You will feel like you are touching tomorrow.

Dear Mary,

I heard you speak about the importance of videotaping your parents or grandparents. Because of that, I now hound my husband and friends to videotape their loved ones before it's too late. That may sound a little dramatic, but when I was seventeen I lost my mom to cancer and my dad died only nine months later of a heart attack. I am now thirty-seven years old, and I would give all that I own to see and hear them on videotape. We have family footage but it is all without sound, and there are only a few seconds of my dad because he was, of course, always holding the camera.

I am sure that it is difficult for anyone with vibrant living loved ones to even think about losing one or all of them. I cannot blame people for not wanting to think about tomorrow. They may not think about the fact that when they do inevitably lose someone dear, they will have to live out the rest of their own life without the presence of that loved one.

That could mean twenty, thirty, or even fifty years. When my mom died twenty years ago not only did my siblings and I lose her, but our children and grandchildren lost her, too, many before they were even born.

Your idea of interviewing and videotaping loved ones is a great one. Not only do the family members get to see and hear their parents or grandparents on tape but they also get to hear stories right from the source. That is the best part. I must say that in our Maltese family with a rich history of immigration, wartime survival, and cultural traditions we would all agree that the "stories" are the part we miss the most about our parents.

Please keep doing your work and encouraging people to pass the stories and wisdom on to the next generation. They really can touch tomorrow.

Thank you and God bless,

Brenda Abdilla

Part One

You are our living link to the past. Tell your grandchildren the story of the struggles waged, at home and abroad. Of sacrifices made for freedom's sake. And tell them your own story as well—because every American has a story to tell.

—Former president George Bush
State of the Union Address, 1990

So you are committed to doing this interview. You can't wait to get started. You are burning with questions, and you have told your elder about how you can help him touch tomorrow. You have done your homework and can envision how absolutely wonderful it will all turn out.

WHEN GRANDPA SAYS NO

I have been there and I can help.

"YOU CAN'T MAKE ME."

Most parents or grandparents will absolutely love the idea of sharing their memories on videotape. But not all. Take my father, for instance. My father initially agreed to the interview. I made all the arrangements and flew home for the weekend. My mother greeted me with the news, "Your father is not going to do this." My dad, an intensely private man, and by his own admission strong-willed and stubborn, had decided to pass on this opportunity. He was afraid he'd say the wrong thing or be too open. Actually, he wasn't sure why he was so uncomfortable, but the safest path was to refuse. I assured him that he could review the taped interview first, and we would edit out anything he didn't like. He appreciated that, but it wasn't really the issue.

I said, "Look. This interview isn't about you or me. This is for generations to come. You are seventy years old. Your sons are taking their own sweet time about making babies, and the grandchildren you do have live thousands of miles away from you. Your grandchildren want to know who you are. They need to know who they belong to. They will want to hear your story."

Finally, I said, "Grandpa Schulte, your father, was your mentor. He passed away twenty years ago. How much would you be willing to pay right now for a videotaped interview of him? How much would you enjoy watching him tell stories of his childhood, talking about his love for your mother, and sharing his philosophy of life?" Dad smiled and walked out of the kitchen. The next thing I knew he was reviewing the questions and making notes. The following day he enjoyed every minute of the storytelling.

"BUT THE VIDEO CAMERA MAKES ME NERVOUS."

For some, the video camera itself may be the concern. In front of a camera most of us are a little uncomfortable at first. After a few minutes, however, my experience has been that everyone seems to forget about the videotape running and just gets into having a conversation. Some elders, however, may not be comfortable with today's modern technology and may refuse to be videotaped. In that case, you may want to simply audiorecord the conversation. If you wish, you could later transfer the voice to videotape and use those wonderful still photos of your family members to bring the stories to life. You may also have other videotape footage of your family get-togethers, and you could use the audiotape as a voice-over.

"MY LIFE HASN'T BEEN THAT INTERESTING."

Everyone has stories. Fascinating stories. Because, you see, stories are just recalled experiences and you can't have lived this long without some pretty interesting experiences. Sarah Delany, the 105-year-old coauthor of *The Delany Sisters' Book of Everyday Wisdom,* said, "Maybe all older people should be asked about their lives. When you live a long time you have stories to tell. If only people ask."

Ask the questions; the stories will come. I guarantee it. In fact, the stories may keep coming, long after the camera is turned off.

I asked my father about his first job. I knew the answer. His first job was his only job. He devoted his life to the Mediapolis Savings Bank. But he answered, "My first job was with Uncle Sam." He began to tell me about getting drafted into the U.S. Navy, his weeks in basic training, his years in World War II as a radar man on a carrier in the South Pacific. He went on and on and on. I sat there spellbound because in my entire life I had never heard him say one word about his years in the war. When I watched his tape I saw the passion and pride with which he told his story and I thought, "Of course he has stories to tell! He was a seventeen-year-old Iowa farm boy, plucked suddenly out of the fields and dropped into the middle of the Pacific Ocean, where he faced life-and-death situations on a daily basis. There must be fascinating tales to tell!"

With the flood gates now open, the memories keep coming. Each year since our interview, when we get together at our annual family reunion, Dad inspires us with more stories. I think Sarah Delany is right. If only people ask!

IT'S ONLY NATURAL

Don't be disappointed if you encounter some reluctance from your elders. Shyness and anxiety may reflect the fact that no one has asked them questions about their life and feelings for a long time. They may worry about their ability to remember accurately. Be gentle. Encourage them to help you. Give them time to decide. Perhaps you could do some "conditioning" for those who are refusing to agree to a formal videotaping. Film them while they're at home doing regular chores like cooking or working in the garage. Show them the tape, and then set it up so they can watch it again after you leave. Who knows? They might even like what they see and decide that doing the interview is a good idea after all. Give them every opportunity to say yes.

❧

THE JOY FLOWS BOTH WAYS

Although I characterized my father as the reluctant one, that doesn't mean my mom did not have her reservations. Today both my parents are very happy that they overcame their anxieties and completed this project. It has been six years since I filmed my mother and just recently I received this letter from her:

Dear Mary,

Even though I always dreamed of becoming a great actress, when you first asked if I would let you interview me on tape, I was afraid to try. But I want you to know how grateful I am that you talked me into it. I feel proud that my family wanted to know more about me. When it was over I felt that you all knew me better, and I remembered myself better, too. Actually it was fun! I am so glad I did not miss this opportunity.

It was good to reminisce after sixty-nine years and to remember the good times with my parents and sisters. I enjoyed reliving my childhood, especially my teenage years when life was not nearly as rushed as it is now. It helped me once again enjoy my own children when they were little. I remembered their teenage adventures and trials and tribulations. I was reminded of how their adult lives brought me the grandchildren I adore so much. I feel good that I have had the opportunity to tell my children I love them, and to give my grandchildren a little glimpse of who I am, especially since I do not get to see them very often.

What I want to thank you most for is this: having this interview was good therapy for me. It brought out feelings that I have not felt for a long time. Sometimes the memories left me a little tenderhearted, but all in all the experience was very worthwhile. Every year on my birthday I sit down with a glass of wine and watch my tape, and I get to enjoy the memories all over again. It makes me feel very connected to my family, those that are here today and even those that have passed.

Thank you so very much for this gift.

Love,

Mom

SET GROUND RULES

Some families may have a topic or two they want to avoid. Just like the stars do on talk shows you can set some ground rules so that everyone is happy with the results. Maybe your parents are divorced and would prefer not talking about that chapter in their lives. Maybe they do want to talk about it and take the opportunity to heal some old wounds. Perhaps they lost a child and would feel too emotional discussing it. On the other hand, they might feel it would be wrong to leave that person out of a family video and would want to be sure to include stories about that son or daughter. Ask them ahead of time. Remind your loved ones: This is not live. If they inadvertently say something they wish they hadn't, or if something comes out twisted and could be misconstrued, well, that is where the delete button comes in quite handy. Assure them that you are their advocate and want only what makes them feel good. Then keep your promise.

One woman told me about interviewing her father. He had divorced her mother years before and had remarried. The parents had not reconciled their animosity and her mother, especially, still felt very angry. Her mother had set a ground rule that she did not want to talk about her ex-husband. So the daughter was surprised and pleased that her father used this tape to answer questions candidly and express his regrets about the hurt he had caused his family. He had only good things to say about his ex-wife and admitted that the hardest thing he had ever faced was his divorce. His children believed the public expression was healing for the whole family and said, "Just having gone through this process has bonded us more closely today."

The interviewer may experience resistance as well. Some people can feel overwhelmed by the scope of the project. Remember that you do not have to do this alone. While one person will probably be the "producer," you can delegate many aspects. Make it a family project. If you are a bit tenuous about the technology, get someone who is very comfortable with it, namely, a teenager. Your high-tech relative will be saying things like, "Oh, it is really easy. See, you just push this button and flip this switch. . . ." Tap into your techie's expertise and fearlessness.

WHAT CAN I SAY? THEY'RE MY FAMILY!

As with many family get-togethers, whether it is a wedding, anniversary, or a Father's Day barbecue, most clans will have some, shall we say, family dynamics out in full force. My guess is your relatives will react to this venture just like they have reacted to family projects in the past. The person who is always responsible for the Mother's Day gift might be running this show, too. The sister who has historically felt left out might feel hurt because she did not get to help select the questions. One brother will watch the tape every day for a week and send the interviewer praise and gifts. His sister will say thanks a lot and mean it, then put the tape in a drawer and not look at it again for five years.

Our families are flawed. They can be quirky. But they are ours. We belong to them and they fulfill our deepest needs. So understand that the interview process might elicit some emotions and discussions characteristic of your family. Just go ahead and do the taping and love them all the while.

TIMING IS EVERYTHING

You will need to prepare for this project by setting a realistic timetable. Give yourself plenty of time to plan. After all, who needs more self-imposed, stress-inducing deadlines? This project is supposed to be fun! Some families will opt for a time when they are all getting together anyway, like Thanksgiving dinner, Christmas, Hanukkah, a baptism, family reunion, or anniversary. For other families those events are just too full of activities, and they'd prefer to schedule a quiet weekend when the interview is the only item on the agenda. Consult your family and get it on the calendar with time to spare.

Connie Asher flew home to South Dakota to interview her parents. Although she feared it was going to be the equivalent of parting the Red Sea, she was thrilled that she could overcome her dad's reluctance.

Dear Mary,

I videotaped my parents two weeks ago. My dad is eighty-one and my mother is seventy-eight. It wasn't easy to prepare for. Dad was extremely nervous and I almost said, "OK, you don't have to do this." But we went ahead, I hired a videographer, and I videotaped each of my parents.

Mary—these interviews made my trip home to see my parents one of the most memorable trips I've made in ten years! We talked more, we laughed a lot together, and I learned so much from them—I thought that I'd heard everything before but I'll bet 50 percent of the stories they told were new to me. What a wonderful experience!

During the five days I was there I know Dad

watched the tape several times. In other words, my parents really enjoyed it, too. And the whole experience was such a great catalyst for conversation and family history.

Thanks so much for the idea, the questions, and for this gift that I now have for my kids and their children to come.

Warmly,

Connie

Part Two

TELLING THE TALES AND
CAPTURING THE WISDOM

Blessed are they who know the way to bring back memories of yesterday.

—Elizabeth Clark

HAVING A HEART-TO-HEART

The big day is here. Grandma is wearing her Sunday best, and Papa is so handsome in his suit and tie that it brings tears to your eyes. Maybe your elder is wearing her favorite kimono for the interview. Perhaps Dad said he would really rather wear his bib overalls, if you don't mind. The key is to make the person happy and comfortable. You are trying to capture the essence of your loved ones so let them decide how they want to appear.

The interviewer's main job is to set the tone. If you act like this is going to be a fun-filled, relaxing, storytelling session, chances are, it will be. Spend some time with the interviewees before the camera starts rolling. Get them to tell a story or a joke and reassure them that is all you are asking for. Here are some tips to consider:

1. *Listen, wait, and be patient.* Don't worry if this doesn't look or sound like a network special. Relax. While big errors can be edited out, the success of *America's Funniest Home Videos* TV show is a testimonial to how much we love bloopers. What appears to be a mistake will seem charming and delightful a few years from now.

2. *Let the video recorder do the work.* All you have to do is have fun. The beauty of the videotape is that you can see and hear your loved one. In years to come, you'll marvel at the way she held her hands in her lap, how his eyes sparkled as he laughed at his own memories, and how gentle and loving her voice sounded.

3. *As you interview, offer encouragement.* The stories will illustrate courage, strength, and hope. Sometimes, the stories will touch hearts. Have a box of tissues and a glass of water handy.

4. *Make the setting inviting.* Ask Grandpa to sit in his favorite chair. Use photos, mementos, scrapbooks, or old letters to help put your relative at ease. Using props can also help to jog memories. Maybe you

have a christening gown, a bowling trophy, a brooch or ring, a favorite recipe, or golf clubs. Perhaps you have the hankie Grandmother carried on her wedding day. For a fun dramatic effect, put some items in a box and encourage your loved one to pull each one out and tell a story. Ask Grandpa to show you his favorite fishing pole and watch him regale the audience with the best way to catch a fish. Even the room you are in can provide props your loved one can describe—the dining room table that has been in your family for one hundred years, or the clock that your ancestors brought over from Europe.

5. *Make it conversational.* Forget the camera and just talk like you always do. Make eye contact. Laugh. If you want to redo a question and you know you are going to edit the tape, just say "cut," pause to give the editor a space, then start over and restate what you wanted to say. You can cut the unwanted portion out later. Do not worry about little goofs. Just keep concentrating on having a good time.

Indy Blaney called me to rave about her mother's audiotape interview. I was so touched by how important the laughter on the tape was. She said, "Thanks for the idea to tape my mother. She has since died of cancer. My father and I recently listened to the tape. You know, Mary, we heard her laughing. I had forgotten it. There wasn't much laughing the last six months of her life. The laughter alone is worth everything."

❧

THE POWER OF PROPS

In the days before my children could drive I spent countless summer hours chauffeuring them all over town. One summer I told them I would be happy to drive them but they needed a "ticket." They could "purchase" a ticket by visiting eighty-five-year-old Nana at her retirement village once a week for a one-hour chat. The day I drove my (then) eleven-year-old daughter Emily for her first summer visit she was very reluctant. As she got out of the car she lamented, "What am I going to talk about for a whole hour?" I said, "Why don't you ask Nana about the dishes in her china closet?" Emily rolled her eyes as only an anguished adolescent could and went in.

An hour later a smiling Emily got back in the car and I said, "So how did it go?"

"I asked her about the dishes just like you told me to do."

"And?"

"It was a one-hour answer."

There was the plate George brought back

from France when he returned from World War II, which led to the story of how they had gotten married before he shipped out but they kept their nuptials a secret until he got home. Then there was the cup and saucer that she bought on her honeymoon, which reminded her that she had lied about her age when she got married (because she was older than her husband), and she did not tell the truth until age seventy-six (when everyone thought she was only seventy). There was the tureen that her mother had received as a wedding gift that . . .

Of course the answer took an hour!

Emily and Nana shared many wonderful hours together that summer, and Emily was thrilled with the family tales she heard, the wisdom passed down, and the family secrets she became privy to. She surprised herself by looking forward to "earning" her chauffeur's fare each week. (No more eye rolling!) She reminded me of the power of using props to elicit memories that warm our hearts.

So go ahead and laugh—be downright silly if you want. Let the person's sense of humor shine through. It will be a thrilling sound tomorrow.

6. *Control distractions.* Unplug the phone, put a note on the door, and turn off the cuckoo clock. Put your pets in another room or outside until you are ready for their appearance. This is very important! The microphone will pick up everything, and even noises that are a normal part of your life will be annoying on tape.

7. *Don't worry about total accuracy.* If your elders relate something that is not entirely accurate, resist the temptation to correct them. If the error is meaningless, just let it go. Listen to how they tell the story: the words they choose, their voice inflections, and body movements. The events need not be in chronological order. You are simply looking for the memories they value. Try not to interrupt. If a story seems to go on too long or the details are a bit rambling, don't worry. You can edit the tape later for brevity. You might also learn some details you wouldn't want to miss and decide to keep that part in after all.

8. *Ask additional questions.* You'll hear stories and details you've never heard before. In fact, the most common response I get from people who have completed their interview is, "I just can't believe how many new stories I heard!" Ask, "What do you mean by that? Tell me more." You might preface some questions with an introductory comment. For

example, "We all know how much you love the game of golf. What was your best golf score?"

HOW TO SET UP THE INTERVIEW

You can conduct the interview in many ways. You might interview your relative in a *Barbara Walters Special* style, with both of you in the picture, sitting together in a cozy setting. Or you can set the camera on a tripod, get the family around the kitchen table, and videotape everything, including the trips to the counter to get another cup of coffee. You may complete a one-hour interview in one setting, with or without stretch breaks. It may take the form of small once-a-week discussions or perhaps a single interview that you add footage to once a year. One relative might do all the interviewing or maybe several relatives will join in the fun. The grandchildren might especially enjoy taking turns asking questions. Perhaps you will want to ask others to tell their favorite family stories as well.

COME REMINISCE WITH ME

You will want to consider the person's age, health, willingness to participate, personality, and the time available. You know your family. Structure the interview to make it the most enjoyable for everyone. Don't worry if you don't follow the interview format

Although I refer often to your immediate family as the interviewees, the idea can be adapted for anyone. Ruth Harthun questioned her aunt and loved what she learned.

Dear Mary,

I interviewed my eighty-eight-year-old Aunt Irene and was so very glad I did. I learned that she was among the first WAC units to go to Europe during the war and how much that assignment shaped the woman that she became. Surprisingly, I also learned a few family secrets. My aunt confessed that she had held a grudge against my mother for over fifty years. My aunt did not want to come home immediately at the end of the war. She was a clerical worker and wanted to stay and participate in the Nuremberg trials. She also wanted to live in Paris for a while. My mother had insisted she come back to help care for their parents because my mother had a family of her own and could not care for everyone by herself.

My aunt is a quiet self-effacing woman and

through our interview I discovered a depth that I did not know she possessed. She has wonderful insights into life and I came away with a lot more respect for this wonderful octogenarian.

Your ideas were a wonderful springboard. I took away lessons from this project that I will always cherish. Now I would like to interview some of the elders in our church to celebrate our church's anniversary.

Sincerely,

Ruth Harthun

precisely. The process sometimes takes on a life of its own. The "interview" could end up being one long storytelling session, as one memory leads to the next. "Tell us how you make your famous cannelonis." "Tell the one about the time you ran away from home." "Tell us how Grandpa threatened to stop the wedding."

I cannot overemphasize the importance of just listening. For the elder, this interview may have special meaning. Reminiscing may allow older people, through storytelling, to reconcile or resolve important conflicts in their life. They may savor some recollections, particularly relating stories of when they were loved. Recalling treasured childhood scenes can be very nourishing. My mother's eyes really lit up when she described how she and her sisters "would put on a show, singing and dancing and doing tricks. We would charge the neighborhood kids a nickel to attend and they would pay it!"

I can see her doing that, too! You may be surprised at how much your relatives enjoy the interview. Let them lead you. Just begin the questioning, let the stories unravel, and feel the joy of belonging.

Dear Mary,

I was a "non-traditional" student (meaning I was nearly forty). One of our class assignments was to interview an older person. My fellow students' concept of old and my concept of old were different. They interviewed people my parents' age who were in their late sixties or early seventies. I didn't think that was old! My neighbor introduced me to her husband's grandmother. Little did I know we would have a treasured friendship.

When I met Hazel Meyers, "Meme" was raking the yard in Reebok tennis shoes. She was ninety-three. She was such an interesting person! She had worked at the Bentley Hotel as a telephone operator. The Bentley Hotel is an elegant historic hotel in Alexandria, Louisiana. Many famous people have stayed there. Meme remembered handling phone connections for President Herbert Hoover. She also recalled relaying calls for General Eisenhower and General Bradley when they stayed at the Bentley.

Historians believe that war strategies, including the D-Day invasion, were made at this hotel.

She had worked at Camp Beauregard, a military training post during WWII as a telephone operator. German POWs were detained at nearby Camp Livingston. Many of them were bussed daily to do chores at Camp Beauregard. Meme often spoke of the German POW she befriended. He was assigned to work in her building. Often she wondered how his mother felt and had empathy for him and his family. This was very courageous on her part because her stepson had been killed in the war. She often wondered what became of this German prisoner with blond hair and blue eyes.

Meme ended up becoming a part of our family. She would call us every night and talk to the children and me. She was very excited because we were Catholic like her. Whenever she lost an item, she would always say, "Jesus was lost and found" three times and then recite the Our Father. She said this novena never let her down. As I am getting older, I

*often say this novena, too, think of Meme, and say a
prayer for her.*

Fondly,

Brenda Tauzin

Part Three

RECORDING THE JOURNEY

GETTING THE TREASURES ON TAPE

The first step is to decide if you will use audiotape or videotape. I encourage you to try your hand at videotaping, but if that is not possible, then an audiotape will fit the bill nicely.

If you choose to videotape then you can opt to either hire a videographer or use your home video camera. For some families, having a stranger in the room will clam everyone up, so the home camera is the best and perhaps the most economical choice. Video recorders have become affordable and amazingly simple to use with automatic features for just about everything. You can also rent one for a reasonable fee. Still, for other families, especially for those of us whose VCRs blink 12:00 continuously, delegating the technical aspects will free them up so they can concentrate on having a good time talking. You might use a combination of approaches such as asking the videographer to set up the camera and then step out of the room during the interview. Or you might use a home video recorder but ask good ole Uncle Harry to man the camera so you can focus on the interview. Each family is different. Think through what will work best for yours.

Following are some rules to make your videotaping a great success. I asked Mark Camacho, owner of 81 Media International and the producer of professional videos, for some insider tips that would ensure a polished final product, and his advice is included below:

- If you elect to use a camcorder, know how to operate the equipment before you begin. Frustration with technical equipment does not usually lend itself to a festive air. (And you have to spend extra time and money deleting those exasperated *+*#* remarks!)
- Use new, high-quality videocassette tape. You will be much happier with the results. After all, this tape is a family heirloom!
- Check the white balance before you begin by verifying that the colors are accurate. Most camcorders have a very accurate automatic white balance feature.

• If you use the date and time feature, use it only at the beginning.

• If you have the option, use power from an outlet instead of a battery. You don't want to worry about the batteries dying just as Mom reveals that big family secret.

• Use a tripod. Otherwise, it will look like your interview took place during a small earthquake.

• Use adequate lighting. Two separate light sources with the same strength are best. Remember: no light, no picture. Check lighting before you begin. Incorrect lighting can make you look old, ghoulish, or wrinkly. Have I got your attention now? Adds Camacho, don't mix light sources. Daylight is blue in color and indoor light is yellow. Either shoot outside or go inside away from a window because mixing the two lights will wash the subject out.

• Change the camera angle from time to time. Just one angle gets boring. Find a comfortable spot to stop, say "cut," move the camera, and begin again. You can easily edit out the cut. Camacho points out that you do not need to look at the camera. Look off camera into the eyes of the person you are talking to. It is much more natural and will give you a feeling of a relaxed conversation versus a documentary.

• Pan the camera (from side to side) very *slowly*. It's hard to pan too slowly. Panning at the right speed keeps everything in focus.

• Alternate head shots (the camera frames just the head) and chest shots (the camera frames the head and chest) with the wide angle. You don't always have to have the whole person in the frame.

• Avoid excessive "zooming." Yes, I know, we paid extra for that feature, but zooming in and out a lot is very distracting to the viewer.

• Whenever possible, reframe or refocus with the camera in "standby."

• Avoid very light, very dark, or very busy backgrounds. You want your subject to stand out, not the wallpaper.

• If possible, rent or buy an external lapel (lavalier) microphone. Check the sound quality before you begin.

• Do a test recording and then play it back. That's what Steven Spielberg does. Camacho says to film at least five seconds before you begin speaking. This gives the editor a little room to work with later.

• If you are using the built-in microphone don't hold or stand behind the camera and ask the questions. Your voice will be much louder than those you are interviewing because you are so much closer to the microphone. Camacho also advises placing the camera as close to the interviewee as possible. Three to five feet is ideal. This improves the sound and decreases the amount of room noise you will pick up.

• Label the tape immediately! This advice sounds ridiculous, but trust me, it's not. When I made my parents' videos I asked my five brothers to make a little clip of themselves relating a story about Mom and Dad. Several of them (I won't name names) sent me the tape unlabeled! When I went to the studio I had a box full of their videotapes that I asked my videographer to add into the film, but we had to spend time (and money) identifying each owner. Unlabeled tapes can easily be lost, inadvertently discarded, or erased. Label them and save yourself some heartache later.

• Make a backup copy as soon as possible. Not next week. Right away. Horror stories abound about the tape that the three-year-old drops in the toilet, the one the dog ate before anyone could get it away from him, and the one Susie records over with today's episode of *All My Children*. These are funny stories if you have a backup.

• Pull out the small tab on the top edge of the tape to prevent someone from accidentally recording over the tape.

• Keep the tapes away from excessive heat (ie., direct sunlight, especially in cars), or excessive cold (ie., unheated basements, attics, or cars in winter).

• Make duplicates from the master (original). The quality of your copy is much better that way. You might consider putting the tape on a CD and putting it in your safe deposit box.

IF YOU CHOOSE TO USE AUDIOTAPE

Your family may decide for many reasons that audiotape is the way to go. Most of the rules for videotaping still apply. I also asked Judy Byers, author of *Words on Tape* and a leading expert on spoken audio to give us her best advice on how to create an audio masterpiece that will last for generations. She offered these suggestions:

• Practice speaking into the microphone and test how it sounds. You may not like the sound of your voice on tape. (It can sound strange to you because when you speak the sound vibrates differently into your ear than when you hear it from an external source.) Not to worry. If it sounds just fine to everyone else, relax.

• Use the best quality clip-on microphone you can buy. You might also consider using a very high-quality microphone that sits on the table or even hangs on the wall. Keep in mind that sound is everything so be sure you do careful sound checks to ensure you are happy with the end result.

• Don't use a microphone that gets passed back and forth. It makes people very self-conscious and it will sound like it on the tape. It is like the difference between a candid photograph and one that is posed. For this project we are more interested in a relaxed comfortable feel.

• Make the recording on good quality tape. Normal or chrome tape is fine.

• Take steps to prevent an accident. If you are using a cassette, punch out the two small plastic tabs on the top edge (opposite the open side where you can see the tape). When the cassettes are "tab out" no one can accidentally record over the content.

• Don't select a tape that is over ninety minutes. A tape longer than that is thinner and not as durable.

• Consider renting high-quality equipment from professionals. They will know the latest and the greatest in gear. Ask for a good time to come in for instructions. Look in your Yellow Pages under "audiovisual equipment renting and leasing," or "video equipment" (many will also have audio). You might ask about using a minidisc recorder if you want the highest possible sound quality.

• Use a dual boom box to make copies. You can make one immediately and send it home with someone else so you have a backup right away.

I had to laugh when Judy emphasized that we should *label the tape!* Apparently I am not the only one who has encountered this problem.

IF YOU DECIDE TO EDIT

The amazing computer age! With the touch of a button, your videographer can "crop and frame" tat-

A VARIATION

❧

Use this book as an inspiration to interview someone who is retiring from your company. Include additional interviews from people who were significant in the retiree's work life (co-workers, the CEO, the night watchperson, favorite clients) and give the videotape as a retirement gift. Title it "This Was Your Life at XYZ Company." Keep a copy in the company library to inspire others.

tered photos, "peel away" to the next scene, or open a red door with the interview "behind" it. Ask! Ask! Ask! You will be thrilled with the delightful options you have, and you will find talented editors world-wide who can help you.

COLORING OUTSIDE THE LINES

A good editor will show you dozens of ways to jazz up your tape. Adding music will greatly enhance the beginning and ending of the interview. You might select your father's favorite song, music from your mother's era, or a heartwarming love song. Maybe you can talk a family member into singing!

It is trite, but true. A picture really is worth a thousand words, especially the old ones. Those photos really make the tales come alive. When my father told stories about his service in World War II, I overlaid pictures of his ship, his shipmates, and a dashing picture of him in full uniform. When my mother said that marrying the right man was the best thing that ever happened to her, I showed a picture of my parents on their wedding day. The effect is dramatic.

You might want to begin the tape with some childhood photos of parents and siblings. You could end it with an array of special photos, including some of the people who will be watching the film. Take a photo of everyone who helped with the pro-

A VARIATION

Ask your parents to tell a story about when each of their children was a baby or toddler and overlay each baby photo as they are speaking. If you looked like your parent as an infant, show both of your photos side by side.

ject and add it at the end when you list the "credits." Everyone wants to be in pictures! Go through that box of photographs you keep promising to put in albums and put them in this film instead. Add pictures of the houses they've lived in, their pets through the years, workplaces, vacation spots, hobbies, or maybe even their favorite chair.

Some families may not have many photos. Scott and Debbie Koop, owners of A Golden Moment Video Productions, suggest using stock footage such as a clip of World War II pilots flying for someone who was in the war or filming pictures from a *Life* magazine to depict a certain event. They also recommend doing a "decade highlight" using pictures and music that were popular for each decade of the interviewee's life. The point here is to put on that thinking cap! Editors like Scott and Debbie can help you be creative so be sure to make your wishes known.

MAKE A WISH LIST

You can add text on the screen, with birth dates, wedding dates, names, or family trees. Another idea is to add some of your old videotape footage to the interview, either at the end of the tape or during the interview itself. For example, if Grandma is telling a story about the birth of her first grandchild and you have a videotape of her holding the baby, it's pure magic. There won't be a dry eye in the place!

If you have the interview recorded on audiotape, consider sending the tape to an editor for a little "clean up" if you think it needs it. She can delete ums, errs, coughs, and other extraneous noises. You can ask her to include audio clips or recorded memories from other family members. But remember, the editor can't remove voices if two people are talking at once, so take turns!

You can select photos for an audiotape, too. You might use the interview as a "voice-over" on video and film the photos that refer to the stories, or make an accompanying photo album. Let your imagination run wild.

Editing gives you endless possibilities. I am a big fan of all that it can add to this project. It is not, however, a requirement. I liked the advice Donna Zebe gave after she videotaped both of her parents. "Don't 'overthink' it. Take the basics and just do it! You may not be a professional videographer, but you can find a way to make this happen. Don't miss out on all the fun worrying about the technology."

So don't let the project get so complicated or expensive that you decide not to do it. As is often quoted, finished is better than perfect.

HOW MUCH WILL THIS PROJECT COST?

Like most things, this project can cost a little or a lot. You can borrow a camcorder from your neighbor, buy a tape for five dollars and have a priceless family gift. You could take your home videotaped interview to a videographer, ask for minimal editing, add a few pictures and a little music, and for a few dollars more have a polished final product. Or you can hire a videographer to film and edit, adding in every known special effect. You can spend five dollars or thousands of dollars. So have a budget in mind before you go shopping. Here are some things to consider.

Interview several videographers if possible and ask lots of questions:

1. What is the hourly fee for filming?
2. What type of film will she use? Hi8, VHS, Super VHS, Betacam, etc.?
3. Can she edit a home videotape?
4. Is there a fee for transferring tape from one format to another?
5. Is there a fee for equipment rental?
6. How much will each copy (dub) cost?
7. What is the charge for filming still photos?
8. What does it cost to add other home video footage?
9. What is the fee to add music? Can you select the music at the studio or bring your own?
10. How much does editing cost per hour?
11. On average, how many hours of editing are required?

12. Can you be present during the editing?
13. Are there ways to control costs (for example, having all the still photos in order before filming to shorten editing time)?
14. How much does voice-over cost?
15. Is there an additional fee for an off-camera microphone?
16. Has she done this type of project before? Ask to see samples.

A VARIATION

Call your local high school or community college and ask for the communications or audio/visual department. A talented student might take on your interview as a school project or he might do it so he can add a commercial project to his resume. Videography student Ben Cover edited my parents' tapes. He did a very creative and professional job and added in lots of extras because he was having as much fun as I was. His fee was much less than I would have paid elsewhere and he included the tapes in his portfolio.

SAVING MONEY

There are also "do it yourself" editing centers in many cities. Check your Yellow Pages under "video production services." Some home video cameras have editing capabilities built in. Check with your local camera shop for details. There are also computer programs that allow you to edit on your personal computer.

CALLING ALL TECHIES

With the Web, the sky is the limit. You can put your videotape on your family Web site along with the sound and send it all over the world. This is a wonderful feature that gets around the problem of different video formats in other countries. Won't you surprise your long-lost cousin in Antarctica!

Steve Heckler, president of WestLake Internet Training, one of the world's leading Web site development training firms, gave me this advice for putting your video on the Web:

"The Web is a great way to share video, as the formats used on the Web are universal worldwide. These formats include: QuickTime (pioneered by Apple) and MPEG3. There are other formats, but only these two are widely used the world over on both IBM-compatible and Macintosh computers.

If you want to convert videotape to a Web-compatible format or vice versa, you'll need a video-capture card (a piece of hardware you install inside your computer) and special video-capture/editing software. For video capture/editing software, I personally recommend Adobe Premiere. (Details are online at: http://www.adobe.com/products/premiere/.

Adobe has a list of leading video capture cards at: http://www.adobe.com/products/premiere/cards.html.)

A VARIATION

Kodak and America Online have teamed up to offer **You've Got Pictures.** You simply drop your film off at a Kodak retailer and check the You've Got Pictures Box on the processing form. After you pick up the photos at the store, click on the You've Got Pictures icon or go to AOL Keyword: Pictures. Then you can view; share; store; order reprints and photo gifts like mugs, T-shirts, and mouse pads; and create "albums" with the pictures. The beauty here is that you do not need to buy a digital camera or a scanner. You just process the film like you normally would.

Some computers (notably the most recent Macintoshes) can handle transferring video to/from tape without the addition of a video-capture card. These computers have a special port (connector) called a "FireWire port" that you would plug your video camera into. There is fabulous documentation for FireWire available via Apple's Web site at: http://www.apple.com/firewire/.

Now some of you are saying, "Cool!" However, if you are still amazed that the kitchen light goes on when you flip the switch you may think that what Steve just said sounds like gobbledygook. And yet you would just love to share your video on the Web. Don't despair. There are people just chomping at the bit (or byte, as it were) to help you. Check in the Yellow Pages under "videotaping and production services."

PUT YOUR HEADS TOGETHER

Let's say you interview Grandpa on his eightieth birthday, and to make it really special you would like to do $500 worth of editing (that's a lot of editing). To finance the project, you could ask ten of your relatives for fifty dollars. Or perhaps you interview your parents a month before their fiftieth wedding anniversary, and in lieu of gifts, each family member makes a donation toward filming and editing and gets a video or audiotape as a keepsake. Maybe this filming becomes a family reunion, Christmas, or Hanukkah project. Keep scheming until you find the best way for you.

Money means different things to different people, but one thing is for certain. When it comes to money, no one likes surprises. So get all the facts you need before you tape the interview. In researching video, audio, and editing services, I was totally shocked at the wide range of prices. The best advice I can give you is to shop around and negotiate. Ask if there are "off peak" prices or other ways to lower the cost.

Listed here are some common ranges of prices. These will obviously vary greatly by locale, operator, and the quality of the equipment.

	Range	Average
1. Filming	$85–250/hr.	$150
2. Editing	$35–150/hr.	$50–75
3. Still photo transfer to videotape per photo	$1–3	$2
4. Transfer of home videotape to another format	$20–200/hr.	$25–75
5. Adding other home video footage	same as editing	

6. Text—1 screen of 2 lines ($2.50), scroll ($3.50/line for first 10 lines) or $75/hr.
   (This varies greatly. Ask!)

7. Special effects   same as editing

8. Tripod rental $5–25/day $10

9. Camera rental $25–75/day $45

10. Microphone rental $20–75/day to $30/hr.
    (This varies widely due to the quality of the microphone. Some inexpensive clip-on models are for sale. Try Radio Shack. Know what you are getting.)

11. Copies from master
    tape (dub) $3–15 tape $10

I paid a videographer sixty-five dollars for filming my mother-in-law's one-hour video and I did no editing. I love the tape. I spent $100 filming and $500 editing my father's video. I love the tape. My friend videotaped his parents with a home video camera and did no editing. He loves the tape. Whatever you decide to spend on this project, I bet you will love the tape.

The end result is a treasure. You can't do it wrong. You can only fail if you forget to put the film in the camera!

Dear Mary,

I've always been interested in my family history because it's a part of who I am today. I had an older cousin, Julie Bishop (actually she was my father's first cousin), who seemed to know more about the family's history than anyone else. She would relate stories that her mother had shared with her. It's the stories and anecdotes about people that really capture their character and traits and "make them come alive" to descendants who never met them. A few years ago Julie came to visit us in Bakersfield and I made an audiotape as she retold stories about the family. I transcribed the tape in 1998 and we held a family reunion for that branch of the family tree on July fourth. I brought a laptop PC to the reunion to make corrections as people reviewed the written document. Several weeks later, I began scanning old photographs and preparing a Web page for this branch of family history. Unexpectedly, Julie became seriously ill and died in the autumn of 1998. I'm thankful that we captured this history while she was with us. Still, I wish I'd asked her a few more questions about her own life.

I think the best part of Touching Tomorrow *is* the sample interview. You pose questions that will help draw out the stories and reveal the personality and spark of the individual. I'll let you know how my next project turns out.

Leslie Klinchuch

Part Four

RECALLING A LIFE

❧

Memories are all we really own.

—Elias Lieberman

GETTING STARTED

Before the interview, warm up. Talk and laugh with each other. Remember, this is not a performance. This is a conversation.

Script out an introduction, if you like, and add whatever pertinent facts and details seem appropriate. Be sure to note the date, location, who you are, who you are interviewing, the relationship you share, and the purpose of the interview. Remember, in years to come, this tape could be viewed by relatives you haven't even met yet!

As an example, I opened my mother-in-law's interview like this:

Hello, I'm Mary LoVerde and this is my mother-in-law, Esther LoVerde. It is November 10, 1993, and we are sitting in Esther's apartment at Dayton Place in Denver, Colorado. I have asked Esther to share with us the stories of her life. We have teamed up to make this recording as a surprise Christmas present for her sons, Tim and Joe. Thank you, Esther, for joining me.

Then I looked into the camera. "She was born Esther Augusta Timm to Otto Timm and Elizabeth Ehlert on July 12, 1908, in Appleton, Wisconsin." I then gave a brief synopsis of her life.

"She is now eighty-four years young. Well, Esther, let's start at the beginning. What is your earliest memory?" Then I proceeded with the interview.

There is obviously no right or wrong way to begin. For my father I simply said, "OK, Dad. I understand it was a dark and stormy night when you were born." He laughed and answered, "A long, long time ago, January 29, 1925." From there it was easy.

For my mom I took a different approach. I began by talking into the camera about her passions: wearing hats, playing cards (she is a master bridge player), and her secret desire to have been a movie star (she'd have been good, too). I overlaid photos of her wearing hats through the years and pictures of her playing cards with her grandkids. I showed some footage of Las Vegas marquees, then began the interview welcoming the "star of our show . . . Lou Schulte!" It was great fun and really helped to capture who she is and how much she loves life.

SELECTING YOUR QUESTIONS

This part contains The Interview, covering all of life's stages. You can use it as is, or you can write in your customized questions and make notes to yourself on the lines provided. Just lay the book on your lap while you interview. Turn the pages as if you are reading your elder's life story. Or, you can use the

---

A VARIATION

Although I prefer one-on-one conversations, sometimes you may want to also interview several generations at once. Let a teenager compare dating rules with Grandma. Ask Grandpa to discuss his view of God with his four-year-old grandson. Sheri Krug plans to interview her three colorful uncles together to record their witty interactions. She said their antics would definitely be worth preserving!

pages you've photocopied and refer to them just like Jay Leno uses his interview notes on *The Tonight Show*.

When I interviewed my dad he told a story about my brother Bill. Six-year-old Bill asked Dad if he could go with him to the county fair where my father was judging cattle that evening. My dad said no. He couldn't watch a little boy and do his work, too. So unbeknownst to Dad, Bill hid on the floor of the old Ford. Halfway to the fair Bill pops up out of the back seat, scaring the daylights out of unsuspecting Dad. It was too late to turn back, and Bill had a magical evening one-on-one with his father. (The rest of us are still mad Bill got to go and we didn't!)

When Bill saw my father tell that story on tape he was so touched. It was clear that this was one of my father's most cherished memories. Bill told me later, "Be sure to mention in your book that parents should tell a story about each of their children. It really makes you feel good."

ENDING THE INTERVIEW

I suggest saving one special question for the end, such as asking about their philosophy of life, how they want to be remembered, or what advice or message they have for their families. The answer is often the most meaningful part of the entire interview. In fact, when I asked people who had completed their interviews they often remark that the best questions were those exactly.

When I asked my father how he wanted to be remembered he said, "As an honest and honorable man." After watching my father's video, my brother wrote, "That ending is a killer—I cried and cried—his words will echo in my mind for the rest of my life."

Lastly, thank your elder for sharing his stories and wisdom. If hugging and saying "I love you" feels right, do it. Years from now you will be glad you did.

Dear Mary,

I so enjoyed this experience that I shared with my parents, and I look forward to sharing it with my mother-in-law. I believe it brought my parents joy to know that I have captured their history on film and that we will enjoy their stories for many years to come. Most important, I believe that I touched their hearts in showing them that their history was important enough to capture.

The entire process of interviewing was a lot of fun. I interviewed each of my parents individually and asked many of the same questions. When the individual interviews were complete, I sat them together for a quick "team interview." It was absolutely incredible. All of the magic that make my parents such a perfect couple came to life, and I got it on video. I brought up stories that each of them told on their own and watched them add to the other's tales and giggle about times that truly helped define who they are today. As I was filming, I could imagine the editing process that would capture their hand-

holding, their laughing, and their kiss in slow motion.
I helped them relive some great moments by asking
the questions, and I'm delighted that I've captured
their love of family and of each other for all time.

This videotape is truly a treasure. I thank you for
putting your ideas in writing.

Bonnie Silverman

THE INTERVIEW

Let's start at the beginning. What is your earliest memory?

_____

_____

_____

_____

_____

_____

_____

_____

_____

I'd like to know about your childhood.
What is your happiest childhood memory?

_____

_____

_____

_____

_____

_____

_____

What were you like as a child?

_____

_____

_____

_____

_____

_____

_____

What did you want to be when you grew up?

_____

_____

_____

_____

_____

_____

_____

What did you do for fun as a child?

_____

_____

_____

_____

_____

_____

_____

Tell me about your parents and siblings.

_____

_____

_____

_____

_____

_____

_____

Do you remember any funny stories about your parents or siblings?

_____

_____

_____

_____

_____

_____

_____

What were you like as a teenager?

_____

_____

_____

_____

_____

_____

_____

Most teenagers do something outrageous or "naughty." What outrageous things did you do?

_____

_____

_____

_____

_____

_____

_____

Tell me about your school years. What did
the schoolhouse/room look like? How did
you get to school?

_____

_____

_____

_____

_____

_____

_____

Now, I'd like you to tell me about your
life's work.

_____

_____

_____

_____

_____

_____

What did you do for a living?

_____

_____

_____

_____

_____

_____

_____

_____

What did your work mean to you?

_____

_____

_____

_____

_____

_____

_____

_____

Did you go to church?

_____

_____

_____

_____

_____

_____

_____

What part has religion played in your life?

_____

_____

_____

_____

_____

_____

_____

How did you meet your spouse? What attracted you to your mate?

_____

_____

_____

_____

_____

_____

_____

Tell me about your wedding day.

_____

_____

_____

_____

_____

_____

_____

Tell me about a fond memory of your grandparents.

_____

_____

_____

_____

_____

_____

_____

What was the best advice your parents ever gave you?

_____

_____

_____

_____

_____

_____

_____

What quality do you most admire in each of your children?

_____

_____

_____

_____

_____

_____

_____

What values have you tried to pass on to your children?

_____

_____

_____

_____

_____

_____

_____

What famous person from your era did you most admire? Why?

_____

_____

_____

_____

_____

_____

_____

_____

I know you've had many happy days in your long life. Tell me about one of the happiest days of your life.

_____

_____

_____

_____

_____

_____

_____

Tell me about the hardest thing you ever faced.

_____

_____

_____

_____

_____

_____

_____

We all have regrets. What is your major regret?

_____

_____

_____

_____

_____

_____

_____

There is a lot to be learned in this life.
What single event taught you an
important lesson? What was the lesson?

_____

_____

_____

_____

_____

_____

_____

What is your greatest pet peeve?

_____

_____

_____

_____

_____

_____

_____

You have seen a lot of changes. What do you wish had not changed?

_____

_____

_____

_____

_____

_____

_____

Who were your mentors? What did they teach you?

_____

_____

_____

_____

_____

_____

_____

What is your greatest accomplishment?

_____

_____

_____

_____

_____

_____

_____

Where would you love to travel to that you've never visited?

_____

_____

_____

_____

_____

_____

_____

What decade of life did you most enjoy? Why?

_____

_____

_____

_____

_____

_____

_____

Tell me about your most memorable illness.

_____

_____

_____

_____

_____

_____

_____

What is your greatest passion in life?

_____

_____

_____

_____

_____

_____

_____

_____

What is the best thing that happened in your life?

_____

_____

_____

_____

_____

_____

_____

_____

We all have disappointments in our life.
What was the biggest disappointment for
you?

_____

_____

_____

_____

_____

_____

_____

You are ____ years old. What's the best part
of being your age now?

_____

_____

_____

_____

_____

_____

_____

In addition to best parts, each age has its
challenges. What's the hardest part of
being your age now?

_____

_____

_____

_____

_____

_____

What would you still like to accomplish?

_____

_____

_____

_____

_____

_____

_____

What important historical events do you remember, and how did you feel about them?

_____

_____

_____

_____

_____

_____

_____

If you had your life to live over, what one thing would you do differently?

_____

_____

_____

_____

_____

_____

_____

_____

What is your most cherished material possession?

_____

_____

_____

_____

_____

_____

_____

_____

What do you fear most?

_____

_____

_____

_____

_____

_____

_____

What would you consider a perfect day?

_____

_____

_____

_____

_____

_____

_____

_____

What is your recipe for a happy, successful life?

_____

_____

_____

_____

_____

_____

_____

_____

What do you want to be most remembered for?

_____

_____

_____

_____

_____

_____

_____

_____

As we finish this interview, what would you like us to remember for the rest of our lives?

_____

_____

_____

_____

_____

_____

_____

Part Five

MAKING IT UNIQUELY YOUR OWN

As knowledge increases, wonder deepens.

—Charles Morgan

MAKING IT UNIQUELY YOUR OWN

The list of possible questions is infinite. To stimulate your imagination, I invite you and your family to review the list below. Check the questions you like and add those to your interview. The nicest compliment I received from my brothers after they viewed my parents' interview was, "Your questions so precisely captured the essence of who they really are." With that goal in mind, here are some ideas for customizing your interview.

1. Who was the best teacher you ever had?
2. What were the dress fashions when you were a teenager?
3. What did you do during the summer as a child? Did you have favorite games? A favorite doll or toy?
4. What chores did you do as a child?
5. What were some of the "old-fashioned" remedies for illnesses that you remember your parents using?
6. How were you disciplined as a child?
7. Did you have any special pets?
8. Tell us about some rights of passage, ie., your first bicycle, your first time shaving or wearing silk stockings, your bar or bat mitzvah, your first date, etc.
9. Did you have a teen idol?
10. Did you move around growing up? Tell me about the houses you grew up in.
11. Who was your best friend growing up?
12. Did you ever run away from home?
13. What were your thoughts when you learned that you/your wife was pregnant?
14. As a parent, what is your advice on raising children?
15. What were your favorite ages of your children?
16. How did you choose my name?

17. As a parent, what were the births of your children like? At home or hospital? Doctor or midwife? Who was present?

18. What was the one thing that bugged you most about your spouse?

19. What was your wedding night like?

20. Tell me about your first kiss.

21. Who was your first love?

22. What was the most romantic event you shared with your spouse?

23. Tell us about your engagement. How? Where? When?

24. What qualities do you admire in your spouse?

25. How do you feel about premarital sex?

26. What factors contributed to such a long-lasting, happy marriage?

27. If you could, what would you do differently in your marriage?

28. Where did you go on your honeymoon?

29. If you had to start over and choose a different profession or role in life, what would it be?

30. Tell me about your first job. Salary? Experiences?

31. You stayed home with your children. Do you wish you could have worked outside the home?

32. What did you like best about your work life?

33. What was farm life like?
34. What are your favorite religious traditions and holidays?
35. Do you believe in heaven and hell?
36. What person made you laugh the most?
37. Who was the most famous person you ever met?
38. What do you wish you had learned to do?
39. What gift did you cherish the most, of all the gifts you received?
40. What were your favorite clothes as a small child, teenager, or young man/woman?
41. Tell us about an embarrassing moment.
42. Recall a funny experience you had.
43. Is there something you always wanted to do but did not?
44. In your young adult life, what transportation did you rely on?
45. What is your favorite food, music, art, movie, flower, and/or color?
46. Was there ever a time when you felt your life was in danger?
47. Whom do you admire the most now? Why?
48. What important historical events do you remember, and what were you doing that day? For example:
    · The Great Depression, 1933
    · Pearl Harbor, December 7, 1941

· Kennedy assassination, November 22, 1963

· The first man on the moon, July 20, 1969

49. Have you ever gone skinny-dipping? Tell me about it.

50. Who was the most influential person in your life?

51. What is the hardest thing about being a widow or widower?

52. What could your children do for you now?

53. Tell us how you feel about retirement.

54. Tell me about the places you've lived.

55. A lot has been invented during your lifetime—from the radio to the Internet. What modern convenience do you most admire?

56. What were some rituals (family traditions) during your childhood?

57. What is your favorite tradition presently?

58. Are there any special stories about your children or grandchildren that you'd like to share?

59. Where are your ancestors from? Tell us about them.

60. Tell us about your children. Was raising children an easy or difficult task?

61. What's the funniest (or worst, most trying, most rewarding) experience in raising your children?

62. Tell me about a memorable family trip.

63. Tell me about your grandchildren.
64. What's the best part of being a grandparent?
65. Tell me about your great-grandchildren.
66. Tell us about the first house you bought. How much did it cost?
67. If you could invent something to help mankind, what would it be?
68. Do you believe there is life after death?
69. If you had three wishes, what would you wish for?
70. What one thing would you like to change about yourself?
71. In what ways has life been good to you?
72. What do you consider nature's greatest gift to mankind?
73. What's the one thing that can make you smile when you're feeling down?
74. What is your philosophy of life?
75. What is the most valuable life lesson that you would like to pass on to others?
76. What was your family's reaction to your engagement?
77. What would be the greatest news you could receive?
78. How do you feel about dying?
79. What advice would you give to the younger generation?
80. Did you ever experience racism, sexism, or ageism?

81. If money were no object, what would you buy?

82. How could I help you live a comfortable life as you grow older?

83. How do you want things handled at the time of your death?

84. Do you believe you have a guardian angel?

85. If you could be any animal, what would you like to be?

86. What do you think was the most important event during your lifetime, and why?

87. What has surprised you most in your life?

88. What sports and activities did you participate in?

89. Tell us about your most memorable vacation.

90. Tell me about your most memorable Christmas.

91. What do you like to do now just for fun?

92. What would be your dream vacation?

93. What was it like to arrive in the United States? What did you bring with you?

94. What was my mother (and/or father) like as a child? What trouble did she get into?

95. What was it like to live in the Depression?

96. What was life like during World War II?

97. What was it like going to war and being overseas?

98. What was it like being at home while the men were at war?

99. Were you in the military?
100. Were you involved in a war? How did it affect your life?
101. What organizations did you belong to?
102. What charities have you supported?
103. Did anything "go wrong" on your wedding day?
104. Do you believe in God?
105. Who was the first president you voted for?
106. What political affiliations did (or do) you have? Republican, Democrat, Independent, or other?
107. Were you involved in politics or did you have political aspirations?
108. Would you like to talk about the greatest loss you ever experienced?
109. Tell me about your college years.
110. Did you belong to a fraternity/sorority?
111. What do you think was the greatest invention ever?
112. What brings you joy?
113. What leadership roles did you play in life?
114. What was your relationship with your in-laws?
115. What one book most influenced your life?
116. What lessons did you learn from your divorce?
117. Do you wish you had had more children?

118. Did you ever triumphantly recover from a great setback?
119. What do you think about most now?
120. What are you most looking forward to?
121. What makes you sad?
122. What is the first thing you tell yourself in the morning?
123. What is the last thing you tell yourself before you go to sleep?
124. If you could go back in time, who would you most like to see from your past? What would you say to them?
125. What do you like most about young people today?
126. What do you like about life in general today?
127. From all your wisdom and experience, what would you change about our government?
128. If you ruled the world, what changes would you make?
129. What is the most dangerous thing you've ever done?
130. What is the most sensitive thing you have ever done?
131. Have you ever saved anyone's life? Has anyone ever saved yours?
132. Did you ever have a near-death experience? Tell me about it.
133. What age would you like to live to?

134. Are you a practical joker? Tell me about it.
135. When you were growing up how were you taught to deal with fear?
136. What is the best part of your day now?
137. What languages do you speak?
138. Did you ever lie about your age?
139. Who is your favorite sports team?
140. Do you hold any records?
141. Did you ever walk a picket line or take part in a demonstration or sit-in?
142. Have you ever visited a psychic? What was the outcome?
143. What was your best golf (bowling, bridge, etc.) score?
144. Did you ever win a sports tournament?
145. What are you most grateful for?
146. Tell me your favorite joke.
147. What do you like most about yourself?
148. What importance do animals have in your life today?
149. If you had a special appointment with the president of the United States what would you say?
150. Money is an important fact of everyone's life. Tell us what money meant to you. Were you a saver? Did money come easily or did you have some years of struggling?
151. Do you remember a time when you stood up for your rights?

152. How are your children like you? How are they different?
153. Tell me about your hometown.
154. Will you read or recite your favorite poem?
155. Do you have a favorite collection?
156. What was the most meaningful award you ever received?
157. How did you choose your children's names?
158. Who were you named after?
159. Tell me about your favorite birthday party.
160. What don't we know about you?

Part Six

CREATING A LIVING LINK

~~~

Memories anchor us to the past, strengthen us in the present, and preserve our love for the future.

—Mary LoVerde,
Stop Screaming at the Microwave!

THE HIDDEN BENEFITS

In 1993, I decided to interview my eighty-four-year-old mother-in-law, Esther. I arrived at her apartment to find her smartly outfitted in a red dress and her hair beautifully coiffed. I began the interview, not sure how she would respond. She was brilliant! She recalled story after story. She told about her life during the Depression when, as a young student nurse, she cared for children with contagious diseases such as polio, diphtheria, and scarlet fever. (The hospital was called Contagion. Really!) She described how many of her colleagues, fifteen and sixteen years old, children themselves, often caught the diseases from their patients and died. She also recalled, with a gleam in her eye, dancing to the Lawrence Welk band in a ballroom in Chicago. Best of all, she smilingly recalled when a surgeon colleague invited her to his twelve-year-old daughter's dance recital. She delivered the punch line like a pro—the twelve-year-old daughter grew up to be Nancy Reagan!

I had not heard any of these stories. On the other hand, I had never asked her.

One of my guiding principles for life balance is that each action should have more than one benefit. (Notice I did not say do two things at once!) My videotaped interview with my mother-in-law has countless benefits. First of all it brought Esther and me closer. You see, mothers-in-law and daughters-in-law have a natural rivalry. After all, we love the same man. My interest in her life stories let her know how much I love and respect her.

After the interview, the list of benefits grew. I gave the videotape to my husband and his brother as a surprise for Christmas. It has become one of their most prized possessions. It delighted my children as well. It not only helped them know their Nana better, it demonstrated that our elders are a library, and all we have to do is ask the questions to hear great wisdom and insight. The tape continued to benefit

Esther and me. I wish you could have seen Esther's face on Christmas morning when she watched that tape for the first time. Talk about balancing my life! And when my husband, with tears in his eyes, said, "Thank you," my Christmas was complete.

One fun benefit came the evening after the filming, when Esther went to the community dining room of her retirement village for dinner. No matter how old you get, you never lose your desire to win at the game "one-upmanship." Imagine the white-haired lady sitting next to Esther saying, "We didn't see you all afternoon. What did you do today,

A VARIATION

When the tape is finished and you are ready to hand out the copies, have a premiere party, just like the movie stars do. Send out fancy invitations, dress up, serve hors d'oeuvres or popcorn. Give your movie a title. I entitled my father's tape, "A Little Romance and a Good Round of Golf," which was his answer to my query, "How would you describe a perfect day?" Ask your elders to autograph the tapes. It will really make them feel like a star!

Esther?" And Esther nonchalantly replying, "Oh, not much. My daughter-in-law just interviewed me about my life and videotaped our conversation so generations to come will know me." I don't care how many times you won at bingo that day, you are not going to top that one!

Esther died of natural causes at the age of ninety. On the day of her death she called the priest to receive the last rites and then, bless her heart, she went to the beauty shop in the nursing home and had her hair colored. She wasn't going to have gray streaks even in the casket! She passed away in her sleep just a few hours later. I was reminded of the day we did the interview six years earlier, when she sat there so beautifully coiffed and dressed up in pearls and heels. What a lady she was! Her tape is now priceless.

IN REAL LIFE

YOU JUST NEVER KNOW

Kay Czarnecki was my friend and brilliant graphic designer for many years and produced the first version of this book, then called *Your Family's Greatest Gift*. On July 14, 1999, she died in a car accident, ironically one day after I learned that Simon & Schuster wanted to publish this edition of the book. I regret not getting to tell her the good news because she was a great champion of this project. On Christ-mas Eve 1999 I received this e-mail from her mother:

Dear Mary,

Thank you so much for your friendship and business relationship with Kay. It meant so much to her.

I will be looking forward to reading Touching Tomorrow. *We recently had a program at our church on keeping in touch, so I mentioned your book and several friends are very interested. There seems to be a great deal of interest in your book's idea, especially with so many of us living far away from our loved ones. I don't know if you know this—Kay came home to videotape us using the book as her guide just ten days before she died. She was so excited about the idea. So this book does have very special meaning to us. Our son tells us that it turned out*

well, but we haven't been able to look at it yet as Kay
introduced it and wrapped it up at the end. It is
rather a twist of the intentions, as she had Patrick
film it to remember us and now we will use it to
remember her.

Again, thank you for your terrific idea and for
your gift of the books.

Warmly,

Carol Moran,
Kay's mom

The hidden benefits of this project never cease to amaze and move me. Little did Kay know that she had found a way to touch tomorrow. On the other hand, maybe she knew all along.

TODAY AND TOMORROW

Many people have written to me describing the immediate benefits of this project. They report how it bonded their previously estranged family back together again, how it gave their widowed mother new reasons to reach out and interact with the family, and how the stories enriched their children's lives. A surprising but delightful benefit was how much the "project leader" enjoyed being the one who gave this gift to the family. Jim Estey wrote how much he loved it when his distant siblings raved about the film and begged for more. I understand the feeling well. One of my brothers wrote to me, "My only criticism is that it is too short! I will always be indebted to you for getting this done because it would not have happened otherwise." What a satisfying feeling knowing you have given a priceless gift to the family you love.

During this project you will gain insights that can make you closer to those you love. When you watch the tape ask yourself, "How can I use this information to make our relationship even better?" When I interviewed my mother I asked her what she feared the most. She answered, "Loneliness." With this one answer she let us know how we can best serve her as she ages. She gets her joy from being with people and the best thing we can give her is a sense of connection with others.

❧

Just today I received this e-mail from Joe Esparza, a consultant from Montana. Joe and his mother certainly illustrate the goodness that can come from opening up to each other.

Dear Mary,

I had a special conversation this summer with my mother that revealed a world that I was truly clueless about. I was able to see the world of a young Hispanic woman who spoke English as a second language, who lived a difficult married life, and then was widowed at age thirty-five. She worked as a meat wrapper, ran a small business, and raised four children. The compassion and closeness I have with her now would not have occurred if I had not become curious about her life and her view of the world. It was one of the most meaningful conversations I have ever had with another human being. My only regret is that I did not videotape the conversation as you suggested. I plan on doing that this Thanksgiving. I hope you can use this letter to motivate people to take the time to sit down and have a truly authentic conversation with people you love the most.

Warmly,

Joe Esparza

I believe that you, too, will be amazed at the benefits you'll receive. It will be an enriching experience
for your elders as they reaffirm that their life had
meaning and purpose. You will cherish the rich treasure of memories they possess. It will be a special
blessing to all who come later.

So get started. Create that priceless gift and feel
the joy of belonging to your very special family.
Reach out and touch tomorrow!

EPILOGUE

I would love to hear from you! Let me know about your experience and what you learned. Did you discover a wonderful variation or pearl of wisdom you'd like to share? Send it to me and I will pass it along.

I would also like to know how you stay connected with your family in this busy fast-paced world. Please send me your ideas, stories, insights, and feedback. You can reach me at:

Life Balance, Inc.
P.O. Box 440276
Aurora, CO 80014-0276
Tel. 303-755-5806
E-mail: connect597@aol.com
www.maryloverde.com

Wishing you a lifetime of wonderful connection!
Mary LoVerde

INDEX

ABOUT THE AUTHOR

Mary LoVerde is a professional speaker, the founder of Life Balance, Inc., and the author of *Stop Screaming at the Microwave! How to Connect Your Disconnected Life.* Dedicated to helping people find innovative ways to blend a successful career and a happy and healthy family life, Mary draws from both professional and personal experiences to connect with her audiences from around the world.

Mary served on the faculty of the University of Colorado School of Medicine for fifteen years and was the director of the Hypertension Research Center. She is currently an adjunct professor at Chapman University.

She proudly serves as the national spokesperson for Camp To Belong, which reunites brothers and sisters placed in different foster homes for events of fun and empowerment.

Mary lives with her husband and their three children in their living laboratory in Aurora, Colorado.